CHIPMUNKS

by Josh Gregory

Children's Press®

An Imprint of Scholastic Inc.
New York Toronto London Auckland Sydney
Mexico City New Delhi Hong Kong
Danbury, Connecticut

Content Consultant
Dr. Stephen S. Ditchkoff
Professor of Wildlife Sciences
Auburn University
Auburn, Alabama

Photographs ©: age fotostock/Takao Onozato/Aflo: cover; Alamy
Images: 31 (blickwinkel), 14, 15 (georgesanker.com), 5 bottom,
38, 39 (Kelly Taylor), 11 (Marvin Dembinsky Photo Associates);
Animals Animals/Breck P. Kent: 20, 21; Dreamstime: 2 background,
3 background, 44 background, 45 background; Getty Images: 8,
9 (Alina Morozova), 18, 19 (Tom McHugh); Media Bakery/Takao
Onozato: 24, 25, 46; Science Source: 5 top, 28 (Richard R. Hansen),
26, 27 (Tom McHugh); Shutterstock, Inc.: 36, 37 (littleny), 6, 7, 12
(Margaret M Stewart), 34, 35 (Roberto Cerruti), 32, 33 (Ruimin
Wang); Superstock, Inc.: 2, 3, 4, 5 background, 40, 41 (Animals
Animals), 22, 23 (FLPA), 16, 17 (NHPA).

Map by Bob Italiano

Library of Congress Cataloging-in-Publication Data
Gregory, Josh, author.
 Chipmunks / by Josh Gregory.
   pages cm. — (Nature's children)
 Audience: Ages 9–12.
 Audience: Grades 4 to 6.
 Includes bibliographical references and index.
 ISBN 978-0-531-20665-2 (lib. bdg.) —ISBN 978-0-531-21658-3 (pbk.)
 1. Chipmunks—Juvenile literature. I. Title. II. Series: Nature's children
 (New York, N.Y.)
 QL737.R68G724 2014
 599.36'4—dc23   2014001509

Printed in China 62
SCHOLASTIC, CHILDREN'S PRESS, and associated logos are
trademarks and/or registered trademarks of Scholastic Inc.

1 2 3 4 5 6 7 8 9 10 R 24 23 22 21 20 19 18 17 16 15

Chipmunks

Class	Mammalia
Order	Rodentia
Family	Sciuridae
Genus	Tamias
Species	25 species
World distribution	All but one species live in North America, ranging from central Canada to central Mexico; the only species outside of North America is the Siberian chipmunk, which lives throughout northern Asia and ranges as far west as eastern Europe.
Habitats	Forests, deserts, grasslands
Distinctive physical characteristics	Large cheek pouches for carrying food; long, furry tails; fur is colored in shades of gray, red, and brown, with contrasting dark and light stripes that run lengthwise along the body; large eyes and ears; clawed feet
Habits	Spends most of its time on the ground; lives in burrows; stockpiles food for winter
Diet	Omnivorous; mostly eats seeds, berries, and plants; also known to eat insects, fungi, and occasionally carrion

Contents

CHAPTER 1

Small and Scurrying

Early one morning, deep in the heart of a North American forest, leaves rustle. A furry head pokes up from a small hole in the ground. The eastern chipmunk quickly looks from side to side as its whiskers twitch, making sure the coast is clear. It then darts out from its burrow and across the forest floor, scurrying beneath the leaves to stay out of sight.

Soon, a least chipmunk makes its way into the area, sniffing in front of itself as it walks. It suddenly pauses, its nose twitching rapidly. There is food nearby! The least chipmunk follows its nose to the entrance of the eastern chipmunk's burrow. Inside one of the burrow's several rooms, it finds a small pile of seeds. Quickly, the tiny thief stuffs its cheeks full of seeds. It hurries out of the burrow and runs toward its own home in a nearby part of the forest.

Chipmunks check for danger before leaving the safety of their burrows.

Squirrels on the Ground

A chipmunk is a type of squirrel. There are 25 different chipmunk species. Unlike many other squirrels, the majority of chipmunk species do not live in trees. Instead, they live on the floors of forests, deserts, and grasslands. Some species can also be found in mountain environments, where they scramble across rocks and cliffs.

Almost all chipmunks live in North America. They range as far north as parts of Canada and as far south as central Mexico, in addition to occupying much of the United States. The only species found outside of North America is the Siberian chipmunk. Its native home is northern Asia, including the nations of Russia, Japan, North Korea, South Korea, and China. Today, it can also be found as far west as eastern Europe. The range of this species' range expanded when captive chipmunks escaped into the wild after being transported to Europe.

Chipmunks can jump between obstacles or from one object to the next as they run.

CHAPTER 2

Survival Skills

Throughout most of the year, chipmunks spend the bulk of their time searching for food. They are omnivorous. This means they eat both plants and meat. Seeds, nuts, and berries make up much of the average chipmunk's diet. Chipmunks also eat other types of grains and fruits, as well as various kinds of fungi. Insects can provide a tasty treat as well. On rare occasions, chipmunks might even make a meal of carrion, which is the flesh of a dead animal. They have been known to kill and eat baby birds, too.

If a chipmunk is hungry, it might eat something right after finding it. But most of the time, when it finds something good to eat, the chipmunk stuffs its snack into its huge cheek pouches. These pouches are located inside the chipmunk's mouth. As the pouches get full, they make the chipmunk's cheeks bulge outward. When the pouches are packed, the chipmunk returns to its home to drop off the food and then continues foraging.

Chipmunks use their cheek pouches to take food or nesting materials home, and to move soil out of their burrows.

Chipmunks in Motion

Chipmunks are fast runners. They can quickly dart in and out of cover, moving from one hiding place to another. Their large, powerful hind legs help them take off quickly. Their clawed feet enable them to grip a variety of surfaces as they move. Each of a chipmunk's rear feet has five claws. Its front feet only have four. The chipmunk's long tail helps it stay balanced as it scurries through its habitat.

Though chipmunks generally spend most of their time on the ground, they are also very good climbers. Some species rely heavily on this skill in their daily lives. For example, the Uinta chipmunk dwells mainly in the treetops. It often gathers food on the ground and caches the food in a burrow, then climbs into a tree to sleep. The Hopi chipmunk is another species that relies on its climbing abilities. It lives along rocky cliffs and deep canyons. This chipmunk uses its claws to grip and climb vertical walls of rock.

A least chipmunk jumps between plant stalks during a snowstorm.

Staying Safe

Because of their small size, chipmunks are often targeted by a wide variety of fierce predators. Foxes, coyotes, and weasels are among the dangerous animals that hunt chipmunks. Snakes are another threat. Chipmunks must also keep an eye on the sky for danger, as birds of prey such as hawks might swoop down to grab them from above.

Chipmunks rely on their speed and small size to stay hidden. They try to stay out of sight beneath bushes and leaves. If spotted, a chipmunk can try to outrun its pursuer. If the chipmunk is lucky, it might be near a small space where the predator cannot follow, such as a burrow entrance or a hollow log. It can dart inside to find safety. As it runs away, the chipmunk makes loud sounds to warn its relatives that a predator is nearby. The other chipmunks can stop what they are doing and hide, so they do not become prey themselves.

*Chipmunks usually hide from predators, coming
out only when the danger has passed.*

Digging Deep

Chipmunks live in homes called burrows. Some burrows are simply holes in the ground or beneath an old log. Chipmunks living in areas with humans might make their homes under a porch. Other burrows are elaborate systems of tunnels and rooms that the chipmunk digs underground.

A chipmunk begins building one of these burrows by finding a tunnel dug by tree roots. A tunnel made by an animal that has since moved on also works. The chipmunk then expands this tunnel into a more complex home. It loosens dirt with its front paws and then uses its cheek pouches to carry the dirt outside. Using this method, the chipmunk creates several rooms connected by passageways. Passageways are usually around 2 inches (5 cm) wide. This is just large enough for a chipmunk to get through. Rooms are slightly larger, with widths of 6 to 10 inches (15 to 25 cm). A burrow might have multiple exits. The chipmunk will often use piles of dirt to disguise an entrance to its home.

A lodgepole chipmunk digs its burrow tunnels just large enough for it to fit through comfortably.

Winter Is Coming

Winter can be a difficult time for many animals. It gets dangerously cold outside, and food supplies are often scarce. Chipmunks rely on their burrow-building and food-gathering habits to prepare. They stay inside their burrows through almost the entire winter. This allows them to keep out of the wind and snow. A chipmunk lines the rooms of its burrow with feathers, grass, and other objects that will help keep the burrow warm. It also uses the rooms of its burrow to keep stocks of seeds, nuts, and other foods that will not spoil easily. This ensures the chipmunk will have plenty to eat during the harsh winter season.

While a chipmunk is in its den during winter, it goes through periods of torpor. At these times, the chipmunk's body uses less energy, so it does not need as much food to survive. In between periods of torpor, a chipmunk might leave its burrow on warmer winter days to find more seeds.

FUN FACT! A single chipmunk stores up to 6,000 nuts each winter.

During periods of torpor, a chipmunk's bodily functions, such as its breathing and heartbeat, slow down.

CHAPTER 3

A Chipmunk's Life

Chipmunks are most active in the morning and in the evening. This is when they emerge from their burrows to search for food. When chipmunks are not foraging, they spend their time resting.

Every chipmunk lives within an area called a home range. Chipmunks are sedentary. This means that they do not generally travel outside of their home range. The size of the home range varies from species to species, but on average it is between 0.25 and 0.5 acres (0.1 and 0.2 hectares). Chipmunk home ranges often overlap with one another. The number of chipmunks in an area depends on how much food is available and whether there are plenty of good spaces for burrows.

Though they might live near each other, chipmunks are solitary for most of the year. They usually fight off other chipmunks that get too close to their burrow entrances. This is because chipmunks will often try to steal food from each other's caches.

Chipmunks have been known to sneak into one another's dens to steal food.

Making Noise

Though chipmunks do not spend much time together, they do have an elaborate system of communication. One way chipmunks "talk" to each other is by making a variety of noises. Each species makes different kinds of sounds. The noises range from high-pitched chirps and whistles to low, rumbling croaks. Scientists are not sure what all of these noises mean. Some are used to warn other chipmunks of nearby threats. Some are used to attract mates, while others intimidate rival chipmunks. Baby chipmunks also use sounds to let their mothers know when they need something.

Chipmunks communicate using body language, too. Their posture and the way they hold their tails can indicate that they are ready to mate or that they are defending themselves. Experts also believe that chipmunks leave behind scents that provide information to other chipmunks. However, they are uncertain how these scents are used and what role they play in chipmunk society.

Chipmunks listen for warnings of danger from other chipmunks in the area.

Many Mates

Mating season is the one time of year when adult chipmunks are likely to spend time together. Most species mate in early spring. This is after they emerge from their burrows and the weather begins to warm up. Chipmunk mating periods are very short. In some species, a female might be available to mate for only a few hours. Chipmunks do not form pairs or mating groups. Instead, a male chipmunk mates with as many females as he can. A female chipmunk might also mate with several different males during the same mating period.

It takes around one month after mating for a chipmunk's babies to be born. Each chipmunk litter contains around two to eight babies. The exact gestation period and litter size vary slightly from species to species. In warmer regions where there is plenty of food, a female chipmunk might mate again in the summer and have a second litter.

Newborn chipmunk babies depend on their mother for food and protection.

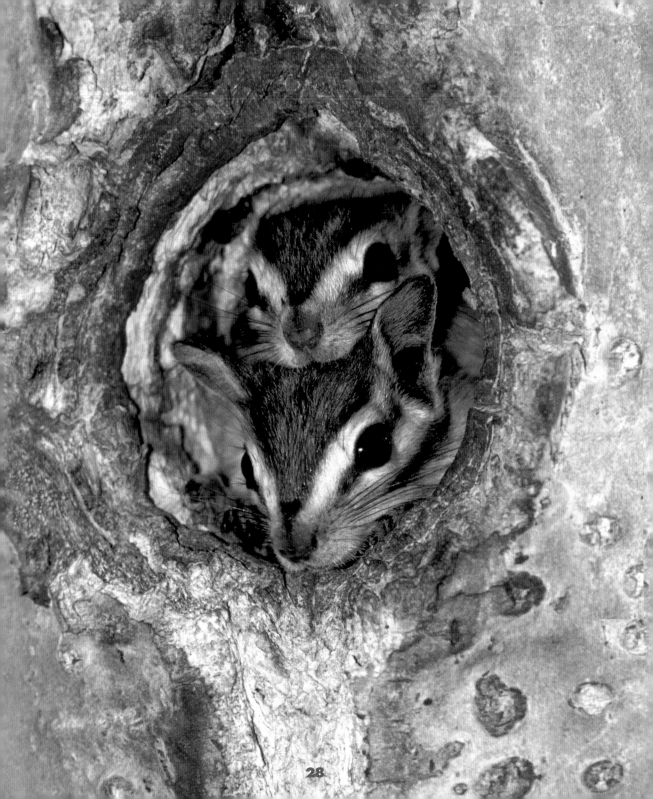

Growing Up

Chipmunks are born tiny and helpless. They are pink and hairless. Their eyes are closed, so they cannot see. Chipmunk mothers give birth in their burrows, where their babies will be safe from predators. Piles of grass and feathers help the newborn chipmunks stay warm and comfortable.

For the first several weeks of their lives, baby chipmunks drink milk from their mothers. The babies grow very quickly. After three to four weeks, their eyes open. As they grow stronger and begin to resemble adults, their mother takes them with her as she forages for food. At first, the babies continue to drink milk along with eating solid foods. They are usually completely weaned once they are seven to eight weeks old.

By fall, the baby chipmunks are ready to fend for themselves. They leave their mother to search for their own burrows and gather food for the coming winter. They will be ready to mate and have babies of their own after their first winter. On average, chipmunks survive for just two to three years in the wild.

Chipmunk siblings stay together in their mother's den until they are ready to take care of themselves.

CHAPTER 4

Rodent Relatives

Chipmunks and their squirrel relatives are part of the order Rodentia. Rodents make up about 42 percent of all mammal species. In addition to squirrels, rodents include mice, rats, and beavers, as well as many other animals. They are classified together based mainly on the shapes of their teeth and jaws.

The earliest rodent fossils discovered so far date back around 56 million years. They were found in North America. These ancient species were the ancestors of today's squirrels and other modern rodents. Experts believe that even older rodent ancestors probably lived in what is now Europe and Asia, but no fossils have been discovered yet to prove these theories.

Many ancient rodent species have gone extinct or changed over time. Today, there are about 2,300 different kinds of rodents living everywhere except for Antarctica, New Zealand, and parts of the Arctic. Of these species, more than 260 belong to the squirrel family.

Rodent fossils have been found in many places around the world. This ancient rodent fossil was found in Germany.

Prairie Dogs

One of the chipmunk's closest modern relatives is the prairie dog. Despite its name, the prairie dog is actually a type of squirrel. It looks similar to a chipmunk in many ways. However, it has a shorter tail, and it lacks the chipmunk's distinctive stripes. Prairie dogs are also larger than chipmunks. They can be as long as 18 inches (46 cm) from nose to tail and weigh up to 4 pounds (2 kilograms).

Like chipmunks, prairie dogs dig elaborate burrow systems with many rooms, tunnels, and entrances. Prairie dogs are much more social than chipmunks, however. Some species live in family groups called colonies. Colony members live together in sprawling shared burrows called towns. The rooms in the burrows are set aside for specific activities. Some hold food, some are for babies to sleep in, and some are used as bathrooms. The huge burrows even have guard posts near the entrances. There, prairie dogs can listen for danger above.

FUN FACT! The largest known prairie dog town spreads beneath 25,000 square miles (64,750 square kilometers) of land!

Prairie dogs live in grasslands and prairies.

Marmots

The marmot is another close relative of the chipmunk. This huge rodent is the largest of all squirrels. There are 14 marmot species. Some marmots weigh as much as 15 pounds (7 kg). A large adult marmot might be as long as 24 inches (60 cm), with a tail measuring an additional 4 to 10 inches (10 to 25 cm).

Marmots are found in a variety of habitats throughout parts of North America, Europe, and Asia. Like chipmunks, they spend winters hidden away in their burrows. Instead of stockpiling food and going into periods of torpor, however, they hibernate fully. Each fall, a marmot eats as much food as it can to pack extra fat onto its body. During winter, the animal goes into a deep sleep. It relies on this extra fat supply for energy. Some marmots hibernate for up to nine months of the year. When they leave their burrows in spring, they might weigh half the amount they did in fall.

FUN FACT! The Vancouver Island marmot is one of the rarest mammals on Earth. Fewer than 400 remain in the wild.

Much like prairie dogs, Alpine marmots live in family groups.
Members take turns watching out for danger outside the den.

CHAPTER 5

Chipmunks and People

Most chipmunk species have large, thriving populations. They are not in danger of going extinct anytime soon. However, there is one chipmunk species that is considered endangered. Palmer's chipmunk is a species that lives only in a very small part of southern Nevada. It is found in a range of mountains west of Las Vegas that is surrounded on all sides by vast deserts. The chipmunks are unable to survive in the deserts, so they cannot leave their small habitat.

The Palmer's chipmunk population is slowly decreasing. One reason for this is that more and more people are using the chipmunk's habitat for their own needs. They are cutting down trees to clear space for new buildings. They are also building campgrounds in the area. This decreases the available space for chipmunks to mate, dig burrows, and forage for food. Because deadly deserts surround them, the chipmunks have nowhere else to go.

As Las Vegas, Nevada, grows, humans take over areas once used by Palmer's chipmunks.

A Small Nuisance

In many parts of North America, it is common to find chipmunks living in the same places as humans. They search for food in backyards and gardens. They build burrows beneath patios or porches. This can cause problems for some people. Chipmunks sometimes dig up seeds that people have planted in their gardens. They might dig holes that can damage flowers and other plants in a yard. Chipmunks can also make a mess by digging through bird feeders and spilling seeds all over the ground.

Some people believe that chipmunk burrows beneath things such as sidewalks and patios can damage the structures above. This is not true. However, people who fear that their property will be ruined often hire exterminators to kill the chipmunks in their yards. Pet cats and dogs also kill chipmunks frequently.

A bird feeder offers chipmunks a very handy source of food.

Good Neighbors

There are many harmless ways to deal with pesky chipmunks that make their way into the yard. Mesh screens can be placed around plants. This helps keep chipmunks from digging up or damaging the plants. People can also remove any hiding places in a garden, such as woodpiles or rocks. Patches of gravel around garden areas discourage chipmunks from entering.

Sometimes chipmunks even manage to get into people's houses. If this ever happens to you, simply open the door and leave the chipmunk alone. If you have pets, keep them away from the tiny invader. It will escape as soon as it can. Like all of the countless animals we share space with, chipmunks should be treated with kindness and respect. Instead of harming helpless chipmunks, you can enjoy watching them as they scamper through your yard in search of seeds and other treats.

With a little planning and cooperation, humans and chipmunks can successfully share space.

Words to Know

ancestors (AN-ses-turz) — ancient animal species that are related to modern species

burrow (BUR-oh) — a tunnel or hole in the ground made or used as a home by an animal

caches (KASH-iz) — conceals and preserves food for use later

captive (KAP-tiv) — held or trapped by people

carrion (KAR-ee-uhn) — dead animal flesh

endangered (en-DAYN-jurd) — at risk of becoming extinct, usually because of human activity

extinct (ik-STINGKT) — no longer found alive

foraging (FOR-ij-ing) — searching for food

fossils (FAH-suhlz) — bones, shells, or other traces of an animal or plant from millions of years ago, preserved as rock

gestation (jes-TAY-shun) — the time when a baby is developing inside its mother before it is born

habitat (HAB-uh-tat) — the place where an animal or a plant is usually found

hibernate (HYE-bur-nate) — to sleep the entire winter; animals hibernate to survive when the temperatures are cold and food is hard to find

home range (HOME RAYNJ) — area of land in which an animal spends most of its time

litter (LIT-ur) – a number of baby animals that are born at the same time to the same mother

mammal (MAM-uhl) — a warm-blooded animal that has hair or fur and usually gives birth to live babies; female mammals produce milk to feed their young

mates (MATES) — animals that join together to reproduce

omnivorous (ahm-NIV-ur-uhs) — subsisting on a diet that contains both plants and meat

order (OR-dur) — a group of related plants or animals that is bigger than a family but smaller than a class

predators (PRED-uh-turz) — animals that live by hunting other animals for food

prey (PRAY) — an animal that's hunted by another animal for food

sedentary (SEH-din-ter-ee) — staying or living in one place instead of moving to different places

solitary (SAH-li-ter-ee) — not requiring or without the companionship of others

species (SPEE-sheez) — one of the groups into which animals and plants of the same genus are divided; members of the same species can mate and have offspring

torpor (TOR-pur) — a short-term decrease in activity that is similar to hibernation

weaned (WEEND) — gradually stopped the reliance on mother's milk for nourishment

Habitat Map

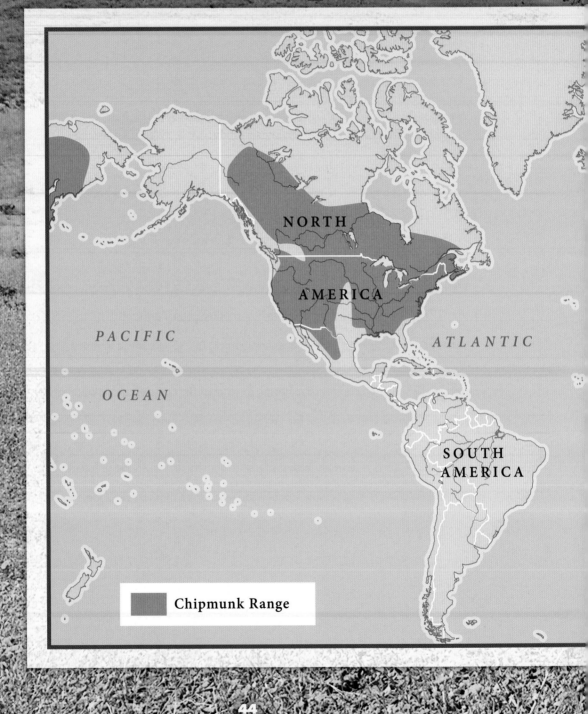

NORTH AMERICA

PACIFIC OCEAN

ATLANTIC

SOUTH AMERICA

Chipmunk Range

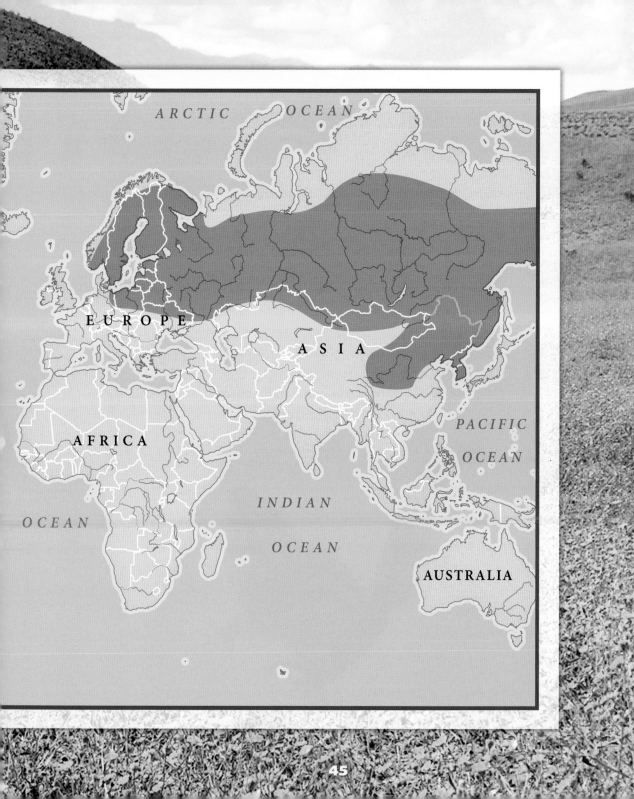

ARCTIC OCEAN

EUROPE

ASIA

AFRICA

PACIFIC OCEAN

INDIAN

OCEAN

OCEAN

AUSTRALIA

Find Out More

Books

Kalman, Bobbie. *Baby Chipmunks*. New York: Crabtree, 2011.

Sebastian, Emily. *Chipmunks*. New York: PowerKids Press, 2012.

Stefoff, Rebecca. *The Rodent Order*. New York: Marshall Cavendish Benchmark, 2009.

Visit this Scholastic Web site for more information on chipmunks:
www.factsfornow.scholastic.com
Enter the keyword **Chipmunks**

Index

Page numbers in *italics* indicate a photograph or map.

About the Author

Josh Gregory writes and edits books for kids. He lives in Chicago, Illinois.